I0401365

Introduction: Understanding AI Communication

In the world of artificial intelligence, interactions between humans and machines rely on a simple but often misunderstood principle: you get what you ask for, even when it's not exactly what you were looking for. This concept underscores a fundamental truth of working with AI—small differences in how you phrase questions or set expectations can lead to vastly different outcomes. And while AI might seem complex, learning to communicate effectively with it can be surprisingly straightforward.

As AI tools become more prevalent in our lives, from digital assistants to sophisticated generative models, it's essential to understand how to communicate with them effectively. This skill doesn't just impact tech experts; it's relevant to business professionals, educators, creatives, and anyone who wants to harness the power of AI.

In this book, we'll focus on two foundational concepts that shape our interactions with AI: prompts and framing. At first glance, they might sound similar, but they serve distinct purposes. Think of a prompt as a direct instruction—a command that tells the AI what you want. Meanwhile, framing sets the context for that command, guiding the AI in how to interpret it. In many ways, framing acts like a mental lens, focusing the AI's approach on the specific perspective or tone you need.

Consider this: if you were to ask a friend to "tell you a story," the response would vary based on whether you were in a serious or lighthearted mood. Without knowing the context, they might choose a tale that misses the mark. Similarly, AI needs both instruction and context to deliver responses that resonate with what you're truly looking for.

Mastering prompts and framing is a simple yet powerful skill. With it, you can shape AI responses to be more relevant, tailored, and useful. In the chapters that follow, we'll break down the differences between prompts and framing, show you how to use each effectively, and provide real-world examples to illustrate their impact. By the end, you'll have the tools to make AI work smarter and more intuitively for you—giving you exactly what you're looking for.

Chapter 1: What is a Prompt?

In any interaction with AI, a prompt is the starting point. It's the instruction you give to the AI, a directive that sets the tone and purpose of its response. Think of a prompt as a question, a command, or a specific request. It's the simplest way to communicate with AI and get it to focus on a specific task. But as straightforward as prompts seem, the details of how we phrase them often make the difference between a helpful response and a disappointing one.

1.1 Defining a Prompt: The Art of Asking
1.2

A prompt can be a question, like "What are the latest trends in digital marketing?" or a directive, such as "Explain the impact of climate change on agriculture." In both cases, you're providing a clear signal about what you're seeking from the AI. Just as a conversation starts with a question or a request, so does any AI interaction begin with a prompt.

But there's an art to crafting effective prompts. If a prompt is too vague, too broad, or too complex, the response may miss the mark. For example:

Vague Prompt: "Tell me something interesting."

Specific Prompt: "Give me three surprising facts about the human brain."

In the first example, the AI is likely to produce something random and potentially unrelated to your interests. The second prompt, however, offers clarity and structure, making it easier for the AI to deliver a response that is both specific and relevant.

1.3   The Role of Clarity and Precision
1.4

The clearer and more precise a prompt is, the better the AI's response will be. AI models rely on the information provided in a prompt to understand what's being asked. If a prompt is ambiguous or lacks details, the AI will fill in the gaps as best it can—which might not align with your intent.

Consider the difference between these two prompts:

General Prompt: "Explain social media."

Focused Prompt: "Explain how social media influences mental health in teenagers."

The first prompt is broad and open-ended. The AI might respond with a general overview, touching on various aspects of social media. The second prompt, however, is targeted. By specifying "mental health in teenagers," you guide the AI to focus on a specific intersection of topics, likely resulting in a more meaningful and relevant response.

1.3 Types of Prompts: Directives, Questions, and Scenarios

There are several ways to structure prompts, each serving different purposes:

1. Directives: These are commands that tell the AI exactly what you want. For instance:

"List five benefits of renewable energy."

"Describe the process of photosynthesis."

2. Questions: These invite the AI to explore a topic or answer a specific question.

"How does inflation affect the economy?"

"What are the latest advancements in AI technology?"

3. Scenarios: These prompts set up a hypothetical situation and ask the AI to respond within that context.

"Imagine you're a health expert giving advice on nutrition. What would you recommend?"

"Pretend you're explaining quantum mechanics to a 10-year-old. How would you begin?"

Each prompt type serves its own purpose. Directives are straightforward and ideal for lists or explanations. Questions are useful for open-ended exploration, while scenarios help to shape the response through a particular lens or role, which can be especially useful for generating creative or tailored answers.

1.5 The Pitfall of Ambiguity
1.6

One of the most common mistakes in prompting is being too vague or assuming the AI will know exactly what you mean without adequate detail. AI doesn't "know" your intent—it operates based on the information you provide in the prompt. So, when prompts lack specificity, the response may drift away from what you intended.

For example:

Vague Prompt: "Tell me about health."

Improved Prompt: "Explain the benefits of regular exercise on mental health."

In the improved prompt, the AI has a clear direction: it's focused on exercise and mental health, two specific areas. This reduces the chances of receiving a generic answer about health that misses the insights you're looking for.

1.5 Exercise: Try It Out

To get a feel for crafting effective prompts, here are a few exercises:

1. Start with a general question, then revise it to be more specific.

Start: "Explain renewable energy."

Revise: "Explain how solar energy is harnessed and used to power homes."

2. Turn a vague command into a precise directive.

Start: "List benefits of AI."

Revise: "List five ways AI is transforming healthcare."

3. Create a scenario-based prompt that provides context.

Example: "Imagine you're a travel guide helping someone plan a trip to Japan. What sites and experiences would you recommend?"

Try these out and notice the difference in the responses. Through practice, you'll see that even small adjustments to a prompt can lead to significantly improved outcomes.

Conclusion of Chapter 1: Why Prompts Matter

Prompts are more than just questions— they're the building blocks of effective AI communication. When crafted with clarity and precision, prompts can bring out the best in AI responses, guiding it to provide exactly what you're looking for. By understanding how to structure prompts—whether as directives, questions, or scenarios—you can tap into the full potential of AI and avoid the frustration of vague or irrelevant answers.

Chapter 2: Framing — Setting Context for Clarity

While prompts provide the AI with specific instructions, framing is the context that surrounds these instructions. Think of framing as the scene setting in a play—it gives the AI a sense of perspective, mood, and purpose, guiding it to respond in a way that aligns with your needs. While a prompt tells the AI what to address, framing tells it how to approach the task. This combination can lead to richer, more relevant responses.

2.1 What is Framing?

Framing involves adding background or context to a prompt, helping the AI interpret it within a certain scenario or perspective. For instance, if you ask, "What are some strategies for a small business to grow?" without framing, the AI may provide general strategies that apply to any business size or industry. But if you frame it with context—such as a specific type of business, budget constraints, or a particular market—the AI can tailor its response to fit that particular scenario.

Consider these two versions of a prompt:

Basic Prompt: "Suggest strategies for a small business to grow."

Framed Prompt: "Imagine you're advising a local coffee shop with limited marketing budget. What are some effective growth strategies they could use?"

The framing here provides more information, focusing the AI on a specific kind of business and financial constraint. This can lead to more practical, detailed, and relevant advice for that unique context.

2.2 Why Framing Enhances AI Responses

Without framing, AI might respond accurately but lack the depth or specificity you were looking for. The right framing helps the AI understand the broader picture, which means it can deliver responses that feel insightful and purposeful. This technique is especially valuable in complex or creative tasks, where nuances in tone, style, or perspective matter.

For example:

Unframed Prompt: "Write a social media post about recycling."

Framed Prompt: "Imagine you're a community leader encouraging families to start recycling at home. Write an engaging social media post that highlights simple, family-friendly recycling tips."

The framed version provides a specific audience, tone, and goal, which can result in a more engaging and tailored response. Instead of a generic message about recycling, the AI now "understands" that it's addressing families and aims to be engaging and practical.

2.3 **Types of Framing Techniques**

There are several ways to frame prompts to get the desired outcome:

1. Audience Framing: Specify the intended audience, so the AI tailors its language, examples, and tone to that group.

   Example: "Write an introduction to coding for high school students who have never coded before."

2. Purpose Framing: Explain the reason or goal behind the response, giving the AI a direction on the expected outcome.

Example: "Explain the basics of mindfulness in a way that helps readers feel motivated to try it themselves."

3. Role Framing: Ask the AI to take on a specific role, such as an expert, teacher, or friend, which influences the tone and style of the response.

Example: "Pretend you're a friendly tour guide in Paris. Describe a day's itinerary for a first-time visitor."

4. Scenario Framing: Create a hypothetical situation that guides the AI's approach.

Example: "Imagine you're advising a single parent on how to budget for monthly groceries. What tips would you offer?"

Each framing technique serves a distinct purpose. Audience framing adjusts the response's language, purpose framing directs the focus, role framing defines the tone, and scenario framing provides situational relevance. These techniques, used alone or combined, enable you to shape responses that feel authentic and aligned with your goals.

2.4 **How Framing Differs from Prompting**

While prompts are direct and instructional, framing is interpretive and guiding. This difference is subtle yet powerful. Prompting alone might give you a correct answer, but prompting with framing gives you a relevant answer.

Take a look at how framing changes the depth of these responses:

Prompt Only: "Describe the importance of time management."

Framed Prompt: "Explain the importance of time management to a college student balancing school, work, and social life."

In the first prompt, the AI may respond with general benefits of time management, such as "being more productive" or "reducing stress." In the framed version, however, the AI knows to address the specific challenges of a college student balancing multiple demands, which likely results in advice that is more practical and relevant for that scenario.

2.5 Exercise: Framing in Practice

To help you practice, here are a few framing exercises. Start with a basic prompt and then add framing to see how it changes the response.

1. Prompt: "Explain the benefits of exercise."

Framed Prompt: "Explain the benefits of exercise for someone with a sedentary job who wants to improve their health gradually."

2. Prompt: "Give tips for managing finances."

Framed Prompt: "Give tips for managing finances for a recent college graduate with a limited budget."

3. Prompt: "Describe the importance of reading."

Framed Prompt: "Describe the importance of reading for a young professional looking to advance in their career."

By adding framing to these prompts, you create a clearer, more directed task for the AI. This often results in responses that are not only informative but also better suited to the specific needs or context you have in mind.

Conclusion of Chapter 2: Framing for Impact

Framing transforms simple prompts into purposeful requests, setting the stage for responses that resonate. By mastering the art of framing, you'll gain the ability to steer AI in ways that make its answers feel both insightful and personalized. Whether you're asking for a basic explanation or a complex creative idea, framing offers a way to refine the response, ensuring that it aligns with your goals and context.

Chapter 3: Why the Difference Between Prompts and Framing Matters

In previous chapters, we've explored what prompts and framing are and how each works individually. But understanding their true value comes from seeing how they work together. Using effective prompts alongside purposeful framing is essential for unlocking AI's potential, especially in complex scenarios. This chapter dives into why the difference between prompts and framing matters and offers practical examples to illustrate how combining both techniques can create responses that are not only accurate but also insightful, relevant, and engaging.

3.1   Why Prompts Alone Are Not Enough

3.2

Prompts alone are like asking a question without any background or context. While the AI may still produce a response, it often lacks depth, relevance, or specificity. This is especially true when dealing with complex or nuanced topics where a simple answer isn't enough.

For example:

Simple Prompt: "List ways to reduce stress."

AI Response: "Exercise, meditate, get enough sleep, eat a balanced diet, and practice time management."

This response is correct but general. It's a basic list that could apply to anyone, without any specific details or practical advice that makes it actionable or personal.

Now let's add framing:

Framed Prompt: "Imagine you're advising a new parent struggling with stress and lack of sleep. What are some practical ways they could reduce stress?"

AI Response: "For new parents, managing stress can be challenging due to unpredictable sleep schedules. Simple techniques like practicing deep breathing exercises during short breaks, incorporating light stretching, and asking family or friends for occasional babysitting help can make a difference. Consider short guided meditation sessions to recharge, even if only for five minutes at a time."

By adding framing, we shift from a generic list to a response that speaks directly to the specific stressors and time limitations a new parent might face. Framing transforms a prompt from a one-size-fits-all answer into an answer tailored to a particular need.

3.3   How Framing Adds Depth and Relevance

3.4

Framing turns simple queries into meaningful, contextual responses, allowing the AI to interpret and approach questions more thoughtfully. In particular, framing helps the AI understand:

Audience: Who it's speaking to (e.g., beginners, professionals, parents).

Tone and Style: How to communicate (e.g., casual, formal, supportive).

Purpose: The goal or outcome of the response (e.g., to inform, to persuade, to empathize).

Here's an example of how framing can add depth:

Prompt Only: "Explain the importance of saving money."

AI Response: "Saving money is important because it helps you prepare for emergencies, plan for future goals, and build financial security."

Framed Prompt: "Imagine you're talking to a recent college graduate starting their first job.

Explain the importance of saving money and provide practical steps they can start with."

AI Response: "As a new graduate entering the workforce, saving money might not seem urgent, but it's crucial. Start by setting aside a small portion of each paycheck, even if it's only $50 a month, to build an emergency fund. Consider creating a budget that includes a specific savings goal for long-term stability and freedom in the future. Automating your savings can make it easier and ensure you're consistently building a safety net without even thinking about it."

In the framed example, the response is not only informative but also practical and directly suited to the audience. The AI understands the person's stage in life, leading it to offer advice that feels supportive and achievable.

3.3   The Power of Combining Prompts and Framing

3.4

When prompts and framing are used together, the result is a response that is both technically accurate and contextually meaningful. This combination is particularly effective in cases where clarity, depth, and empathy are needed. Let's look at a few examples of how combining prompts and framing can improve AI output:

1. Example 1: Creating Engaging Content

Prompt Only: "Write a blog post about healthy eating."

Framed Prompt: "Write a blog post about healthy eating for young professionals who are always on the go. Focus on quick, nutritious meal ideas that require minimal preparation."

AI Response: "For busy young professionals, healthy eating can feel like a challenge, but with a few smart choices, it's easier than you think. Here are five quick, nutritious meals that can be prepared in under 15 minutes..."

With framing, the response is tailored to a specific audience, making it more engaging and directly applicable to their lifestyle.

2. Example 2: Providing Practical Advice

Prompt Only: "Give advice on improving productivity."

Framed Prompt: "Imagine you're advising a remote worker struggling with distractions at home. What are some strategies they could use to improve their productivity?"

AI Response: "For remote workers facing distractions, setting up a designated workspace can make a big difference. Establish a daily routine, use noise-canceling headphones, and consider techniques like the Pomodoro method to structure work time with short breaks. Limiting social media access during work hours can also help minimize interruptions."

In this case, framing helps the AI to deliver advice that feels realistic and relevant to the specific challenges faced by remote workers, rather than offering generic productivity tips.

3.5 Common Scenarios Where Framing Makes a Difference

3.6

Framing can enhance responses across a variety of scenarios, including:

Education: Asking AI to explain complex topics to beginners, students, or children in age-appropriate language.

Business: Framing AI to think from a startup's or small business's perspective, leading to more practical advice.

Creative Writing: Providing creative or narrative context, such as setting a tone, genre, or character point of view, to guide storytelling.

Customer Service: Shaping responses to empathize with customer concerns or answer in a friendly, supportive manner.

In each of these areas, framing transforms AI from a simple information provider to a conversational assistant that understands context and can communicate with nuance and empathy.

3.5   Practical Tips for Mastering Prompts and Framing

3.6

Now that we've explored the difference between prompts and framing, here are some practical tips to help you master both techniques:

1. Be Specific with Your Audience: Think about who the information is for. Providing audience context can greatly enhance the relevance of the AI's response.

2. Define the Goal of the Response: Specify whether you want to inform, persuade, entertain, or support. This helps the AI strike the right tone and approach.

3. Use Scenarios to Add Realism: Framing with a scenario creates a story-like context that the AI can follow, leading to responses that feel more authentic and actionable.

4. Combine Prompts and Framing for Complex Tasks: For nuanced topics, pair a clear prompt with detailed framing. This gives the AI both structure and depth, leading to responses that are accurate and engaging.

5. Experiment and Refine: Don't be afraid to rephrase or add more framing if the initial response isn't quite right. AI interactions often improve with slight adjustments.

Conclusion of Chapter 3: Why It Matters

The difference between prompts and framing is more than just a matter of wording; it's about transforming AI into a tool that understands the full scope of your request. By blending effective prompts with purposeful framing, you can guide AI to respond in ways that are insightful, tailored, and meaningful. The impact goes beyond just getting "better answers"—it's about getting answers that feel right for you and your needs.

Chapter 4: Crafting Effective Prompts and Frames

In previous chapters, we've covered the basics of prompts and framing and why their difference matters. Now, we're diving into practical techniques to help you craft effective prompts and frames together. This chapter will guide you through methods to optimize your AI interactions, providing strategies and examples for different types of tasks. Whether you're looking to enhance productivity, generate creative content, or solve specific problems, mastering the art of combining prompts and frames can help you get precisely what you need from AI.

4.1 Key Principles for Crafting Effective Prompts and Frames

4.2

To create responses that feel relevant and purposeful, follow these core principles:

1. Clarity: Clearly state what you need. Avoid vague or overly broad language.

2. Specificity: Be specific about the details you want AI to focus on, whether it's a topic, audience, or style.

3. Relevance: Ensure that your framing aligns with the type of response you're seeking. Consider the outcome you desire and craft the frame accordingly.

4. Adaptability: Test different approaches and adjust your prompt or frame as needed if the response isn't quite what you envisioned.

4.2   Step-by-Step Guide to Building Prompts and Frames

4.3

Building an effective prompt with framing can be broken down into a few steps. Let's go through each step with examples.

Step 1: Define Your Goal

The first step is to clarify your goal. Ask yourself what outcome you're aiming for. This could be to inform, inspire, persuade, or entertain. Having a clear goal helps set the tone and guides your prompt.

Example Goal: "I want to create a motivational message for young entrepreneurs starting their own business."

Step 2: Choose the Right Prompt Type

Next, decide whether your prompt is best structured as a directive, question, or scenario. Choose based on the level of detail you need and the type of response you're seeking.

Directive Prompt: "List five motivational tips for young entrepreneurs starting their own business."

Question Prompt: "What are some key strategies for young entrepreneurs facing challenges in business?"

Scenario Prompt: "Imagine you're a mentor giving advice to a young entrepreneur facing their first major setback. What would you say?"

Choosing a prompt type is critical as it shapes how AI approaches your question or task.

Step 3: Add Framing for Context

Once you have a prompt, it's time to frame it with context to shape the response. Consider adding details about the audience, tone, style, or scenario.

Framed Prompt: "Imagine you're a seasoned entrepreneur speaking to a group of recent college graduates who are launching their first startup. Provide five motivational tips that are practical and encouraging for young entrepreneurs facing tough competition."

Here, the framing specifies the audience (recent college graduates), purpose (motivation), and context (facing competition), which helps the AI generate a response that feels personal and tailored to the situation.

Step 4: Refine and Test the Prompt and Frame Together

Testing and refining are crucial, especially if your first attempt doesn't yield the desired outcome. Small tweaks to the wording, details, or scenario can improve relevance and accuracy.

For example, if the response is too general, you might add more framing:

Original Framed Prompt: "Give five motivational tips for young entrepreneurs facing competition."

Refined Framed Prompt: "Imagine you're a startup coach speaking to young entrepreneurs in the tech industry. Provide five practical tips for staying motivated while competing against established companies."

Adding "in the tech industry" further narrows the context, guiding the AI to respond with industry-specific insights.

4.4   Examples of Effective Prompts and Frames for Different Tasks

4.5

Let's look at how to apply these techniques to various types of tasks.

Example 1: Educational Content

Goal: To explain a complex concept in simple terms for beginners.

Prompt Only: "Explain quantum mechanics."

Framed Prompt: "Imagine you're a high school science teacher explaining quantum mechanics to students encountering the concept for the first time. Use simple language and relatable examples."

Expected Outcome: The AI is more likely to provide a clear, accessible explanation with relatable examples, making a difficult subject easier to understand for beginners.

Example 2: Creative Writing

Goal: To generate a vivid scene for a fantasy story.

Prompt Only: "Describe a magical forest."

Framed Prompt: "Imagine you're a narrator in a fantasy story describing a magical forest where every tree glows faintly under the light of a full moon. Describe the sights, sounds, and atmosphere to create an enchanting setting."

Expected Outcome: With the framing, the AI is likely to create a detailed and immersive description, including sensory details like light, sound, and mood, enhancing the scene's magical quality.

Example 3: Business Advice

Goal: To provide practical marketing strategies for a small business.

Prompt Only: "Suggest marketing strategies for a small business."

Framed Prompt: "Imagine you're advising a small, family-owned bakery with a limited budget and strong community ties. Provide five affordable, effective marketing strategies they can implement to attract more local customers."

Expected Outcome: The response will likely focus on budget-friendly, community-based marketing strategies that are tailored to a small bakery's needs, such as collaborating with local businesses or promoting on social media.

Example 4: Personal Development

Goal: To encourage someone who is struggling with self-doubt.

Prompt Only: "Give advice on overcoming self-doubt."

Framed Prompt: "Imagine you're a supportive friend giving advice to someone experiencing self-doubt at the beginning of a new career. Offer practical steps and encouragement."

Expected Outcome: The AI is guided to respond in a warm, empathetic tone, providing gentle, actionable steps for overcoming self-doubt, which feels more personal and supportive than a general list of tips.

4.3　Advanced Techniques for Effective Prompting and Framing

4.4

Once you're comfortable with basic prompting and framing, you can try more advanced techniques to refine the AI's responses further.

1. Use Comparisons and Analogies: Framing with analogies can help clarify complex topics.

   Example: "Explain blockchain technology as if it's a digital ledger that works like a shared notebook among friends, where everyone can see each entry but no one can erase it."

2. Role-Play Scenarios for Deeper Engagement: Setting the AI in a role can add authenticity to the response.

Example: "Pretend you're a career coach advising a mid-career professional on how to make a successful career transition into a new industry."

3. Incorporate Specific Timeframes or Settings: Adding timeframes can give AI guidance on tone or urgency.

Example: "Provide five tips for achieving work-life balance in a high-stress job, focusing on small steps someone could take each day."

4. Limit or Expand the Scope with Constraints: Constrain or broaden the scope to suit your needs.

Example: "List three quick strategies for improving public speaking skills that can be practiced in under 10 minutes each."

4.5 Practice Exercises: Try Crafting Your Own

4.6

To strengthen your prompting and framing skills, here are some exercises. Start with a basic prompt, then add layers of framing.

1. Prompt: "Give advice on public speaking."

Framed Prompt: "Imagine you're coaching someone with a big presentation next week who's never spoken in public before. Provide advice to help them feel confident and prepared."

2. Prompt: "Explain the benefits of meditation."

Framed Prompt: "Describe the benefits of meditation to a busy professional looking for simple ways to reduce stress and focus better throughout the day."

3. Prompt: "Provide tips on managing time."

Framed Prompt: "Imagine you're advising a college student juggling classes, a part-time job, and extracurricular activities. What are some practical time management tips they can use?"

By practicing with different scenarios, you can see how small adjustments in framing can lead to responses that feel much more relevant and customized.

Conclusion of Chapter 4: The Art of Prompting and Framing

Crafting effective prompts and frames is an art, one that grows easier and more intuitive with practice. By following these steps—defining your goal, choosing the right prompt type, adding framing, and refining as needed—you'll gain a deeper understanding of how to communicate with AI to achieve tailored, valuable responses. With the right balance of clarity, context, and adaptability, you'll be able to unlock the full potential of AI for a wide range of applications.

Chapter 5: Common Mistakes and How to Avoid Them

Even with a solid understanding of prompts and framing, it's easy to make mistakes that lead to vague, inaccurate, or irrelevant AI responses. In this chapter, we'll examine the most common mistakes people make when interacting with AI and provide practical strategies to avoid them. By identifying these pitfalls, you'll be better equipped to create effective prompts and frames, saving time and improving the quality of your interactions.

5.1 Common Mistake #1: Being Too Vague

5.2

Problem: Vague prompts give the AI little guidance on what you actually need, often leading to generic or incomplete responses.

Example of Vague Prompt: "Tell me about climate change."

AI Response: The response may be broad, covering basic information that doesn't address any specific question or angle.

Solution: Add specificity by focusing on a particular aspect, perspective, or audience. Include relevant details, such as the purpose or intended outcome of the response.

Improved Prompt: "Explain the impact of climate change on coastal cities, focusing on the economic risks."

By specifying "economic risks" and "coastal cities," you give the AI a clear direction, resulting in a more targeted and relevant response.

5.3   Common Mistake #2: Asking Compound Questions

5.4

Problem: Compound questions, or prompts that ask multiple things at once, can confuse the AI, resulting in incomplete or scattered answers.

Example of Compound Prompt: "Explain the benefits of exercise, how it affects mental health, and how often someone should exercise each week."

Solution: Break down compound prompts into simpler, single-focused questions. This helps the AI address each question thoroughly, leading to clearer responses.

Improved Prompts:

"Explain the general benefits of exercise."

"Describe how exercise impacts mental health."

"How often should someone exercise each week for optimal health?"

By separating each question, you make it easier for the AI to respond with depth and clarity.

5.3 Common Mistake #3: Forgetting to Add Framing for Context

Problem: Without context, the AI may respond with information that's correct but not relevant to your needs. A lack of framing can make responses feel generic or disconnected.

Example of Prompt Without Framing: "Give tips on productivity."

AI Response: The AI might respond with general productivity tips that aren't specific to any job, lifestyle, or audience.

Solution: Add context by specifying an audience, setting, or purpose to help the AI tailor its response.

Improved Prompt with Framing: "Imagine you're advising a remote worker who faces frequent distractions at home. Provide tips to improve productivity."

Adding this context guides the AI to focus on productivity strategies suited to remote workers, making the advice more applicable and useful.

5.5 Common Mistake #4: Overloading with Too Much Detail

5.6

Problem: While framing is valuable, providing too many details can make prompts confusing or restrictive, leading the AI to focus on minor points rather than the main goal.

Example of Overly Detailed Prompt: "Imagine you're a nutritionist speaking to a group of college students. Explain the benefits of eating fruits and vegetables, but also cover protein, carbohydrates, vitamins, meal planning, hydration, and how they can fit these into a tight budget."

Solution: Focus on the core message or primary question, then add one or two framing details that guide the response.

Improved Prompt: "Imagine you're a nutritionist speaking to college students on a budget. Explain the benefits of eating fruits and vegetables and offer practical tips for incorporating them affordably."

This focused prompt still provides context but avoids overloading the AI, allowing for a concise, relevant response.

5.5 Common Mistake #5: Using Jargon or Ambiguous Language

Problem: Using jargon, slang, or overly complex language can confuse the AI, leading to responses that don't align with your expectations.

Example of Jargon-Heavy Prompt: "Describe the UX ROI when implementing A/B testing in B2B SaaS onboarding."

AI Response: The AI may misunderstand the terms, leading to unclear or incomplete explanations.

Solution: Simplify language and clarify any specialized terms. If technical terms are essential, provide a brief definition within the prompt.

Improved Prompt: "Explain how A/B testing can improve user experience and increase return on investment for a B2B software company during the onboarding process."

This version is easier for the AI to interpret, resulting in a response that's clear and relevant.

5.7 Common Mistake #6: Neglecting Tone and Style

5.8

Problem: Failing to specify tone and style can lead to responses that feel off-brand or don't fit the intended audience. For example, a business prompt might return a casual tone when a formal tone is required.

Example of Prompt Without Tone Specification: "Write an introduction to a business report on market trends."

AI Response: The response might be too informal, lacking the professionalism expected in a business report.

Solution: Specify the desired tone and style, whether it's formal, conversational, motivational, or academic.

Improved Prompt: "Write a formal introduction for a business report on current market trends, suitable for executives."

By clarifying the tone, you ensure the response aligns with professional standards and expectations.

5.7 Common Mistake #7: Ignoring AI's Limitations

Problem: Expecting too much from AI can lead to frustration, especially when asking for highly nuanced, subjective, or creative responses that require human judgment.

Example of Overly Complex Prompt: "Write an in-depth psychological analysis of a character's motivations in a novel."

Solution: Be aware of the limitations of AI and adjust expectations accordingly. When possible, guide the AI with specific points to cover, knowing that it can provide insights but may not fully replicate human expertise.

Improved Prompt: "Provide a basic analysis of a character's motivations in a novel, focusing on key actions and likely reasons behind them."

Recognizing these limitations helps you create prompts that the AI can realistically and accurately respond to.

5.9   Quick Tips for Effective Prompting and Framing

5.10

Here's a summary of practical tips to help avoid common mistakes:

1. Be Specific: Add detail without overwhelming the prompt. Focus on what's essential.

2. Avoid Compound Prompts: Break down complex prompts into multiple questions.

3. Use Framing Thoughtfully: Add context that's directly relevant to the response you want.

4. Simplify Language: Avoid jargon or unclear terms unless necessary, and define terms when needed.

5. Specify Tone and Style: Guide the AI's response by choosing an appropriate tone.

6. Know the AI's Limits: Keep expectations realistic, especially for tasks that require human insight.

5.9 **Practice Exercises: Spotting and Fixing Mistakes**

To reinforce these concepts, try these exercises. Read each prompt, identify the mistake, and rewrite it for improvement.

1. Prompt: "Explain the importance of financial planning for someone who wants to retire."

Issue: Too vague. Specify the age or situation of the person.

Improved Prompt: "Imagine you're advising someone in their 30s who wants to retire early. Explain the importance of financial planning and provide practical steps they can take now."

2. Prompt: "What are the benefits of exercise for mental health, and how often should one exercise weekly?"

Issue: Compound question.

Improved Prompts:

"Explain how exercise benefits mental health."

"How often should one exercise each week to improve mental health?"

3. Prompt: "Give me some tips on time management."

Issue: Lacks framing and specificity.

Improved Prompt: "Provide time management tips for a graduate student balancing a part-time job, classes, and study time."

4. Prompt: "Write a motivational speech for a business audience."

Issue: No specified tone, audience, or focus.

Improved Prompt: "Write a motivational speech for a team of sales professionals, encouraging them to stay resilient and focused on goals during challenging times."

By practicing these exercises, you'll develop a habit of refining prompts and frames, leading to more accurate and relevant AI responses.

Conclusion of Chapter 5: Avoiding Common Mistakes

Effective prompting and framing are skills that improve with practice, especially as you become more aware of common pitfalls. By avoiding vagueness, using framing thoughtfully, and specifying tone and purpose, you'll gain greater control over the quality of AI responses. Each adjustment, no matter how small, contributes to a more valuable interaction.

Chapter 6: Becoming a Skilled AI User

Now that you've learned the fundamentals of prompting and framing, it's time to bring everything together to develop advanced skills for interacting with AI. Being a skilled AI user goes beyond understanding concepts—it involves applying strategies with creativity, patience, and adaptability. In this chapter, we'll cover how to use your new skills effectively in various real-world scenarios, offering tips to help you master AI communication across different fields and purposes.

6.1 Embracing a Strategic Approach

Using AI successfully requires a strategic approach. Skilled AI users know that each interaction is an opportunity to refine techniques and explore new possibilities. Here are some strategies to keep in mind:

Set Clear Objectives: Always start with a clear goal for your interaction. Knowing exactly what you want helps guide the AI to a relevant and focused response.

Think Iteratively: AI interactions often improve over multiple attempts. Adjust prompts and framing as needed, experimenting with slight variations until you achieve the desired outcome.

Reflect on Responses: Take a moment to evaluate each response, considering whether it aligns with your original goal. This reflection can reveal insights about how to refine your approach in future interactions.

6.2 Adapting to Different Contexts and Audiences

One of the most valuable skills an AI user can develop is adaptability. Your approach may need to change based on the context, audience, or type of response you're looking for. Let's look at how to adapt prompts and framing across different scenarios:

Educational Content

When creating educational content, clarity and accessibility are key. Use prompts and frames that simplify complex topics and adapt language for the intended audience.

Example: "Explain photosynthesis to a 5th-grade science class using simple language and examples."

Approach: Focus on breaking down concepts and avoiding technical jargon. Test responses for age-appropriate language.

Professional Advice

For professional settings, adopt a tone that matches the level of expertise of your audience. Whether you're seeking advice or generating content for colleagues, framing for professionalism can elevate the response.

Example: "Imagine you're advising a mid-level marketing manager on developing a digital campaign for a new product launch. Provide practical, actionable steps."

Approach: Keep the response focused on real-world applications, step-by-step strategies, and insights that match the expected knowledge level.

Creative Writing

In creative contexts, framing plays an essential role in inspiring the AI to produce imaginative, original responses. Use prompts that offer rich descriptions or unique scenarios to set the stage.

Example: "Write a short story introduction about a world where music has the power to control the weather."

Approach: Encourage the AI to engage in world-building by specifying sensory details, character emotions, and setting.

Customer Support and Empathy

If you're using AI to provide customer support or guidance, it's important to frame responses with empathy and a customer-centered approach. Focus on tone, friendliness, and clarity.

Example: "Imagine you're a customer service representative helping a frustrated customer who received a damaged item. Write a response that empathizes with their situation and offers a solution."

Approach: Use framing to set a warm, understanding tone and guide the AI toward a response that acknowledges the customer's feelings while offering actionable help.

6.3 **Fine-Tuning for Optimal Results**

To get the best results, skilled AI users learn how to fine-tune responses by experimenting with:

Word Choice: Small changes in word choice can alter tone or emphasis. For instance, using "explore" instead of "describe" can encourage a more open-ended and creative response.

Prompt Length: Sometimes, longer prompts with detailed framing yield better answers, while shorter prompts work for simple requests. Experiment with both to see what works best.

Iterative Refinement: After receiving an initial response, refine the prompt or framing based on the AI's interpretation. This iterative approach often results in increasingly accurate and relevant responses.

6.4 **Leveraging AI's Strengths and Compensating for Limitations**

Being a skilled AI user means understanding the strengths and limitations of AI, then leveraging both to your advantage. Here are some tips for balancing these aspects:

Strengths:

Data-Driven Insights: AI excels at processing vast amounts of information quickly. Use it for research, summaries, and data analysis.

Consistency and Repetition: AI can provide consistent responses, making it useful for tasks that require standardization, such as customer support responses or FAQs.

Limitations:

Nuance and Subjectivity: AI may struggle with highly subjective or complex tasks that require deep emotional understanding. For these tasks, be specific in framing and add context where possible.

Creative Originality: While AI can assist in generating ideas, creative depth may require human oversight. Use AI-generated responses as a foundation, then add your own unique perspective or revisions.

6.5 Practice Exercises: Applying Skills Across Different Scenarios

Here are some exercises to help you put your skills into practice. Use prompts and framing to guide the AI's response in each scenario, aiming to achieve a relevant and insightful outcome.

1. Educational Scenario: You're creating a lesson for high school students about the impact of climate change.

Prompt: "Explain the impact of climate change on the ocean in simple terms suitable for high school students. Include examples of how it affects marine life."

Approach: Focus on clarity and relatability, with examples that resonate with teenagers.

2. Business Scenario: You need ideas for a social media campaign for a small bakery.

Prompt: "Imagine you're a marketing consultant advising a small, family-owned bakery. Suggest five social media campaign ideas that would engage a local audience."

Approach: Tailor responses to the bakery's local market and emphasize community engagement.

3. Creative Writing Scenario: You're brainstorming a fantasy character.

Prompt: "Describe a character in a fantasy novel who is known for their ability to communicate with animals. Include details about their personality, appearance, and unique abilities."

Approach: Frame for sensory and descriptive details to help build a vivid character profile.

4. Customer Support Scenario: You need to write a response to a customer who is upset about a late delivery.

Prompt: "Imagine you're a customer service representative addressing a customer's frustration over a delayed delivery. Write a response that empathizes with their inconvenience and offers a solution."

Approach: Use framing to create an empathetic tone and focus on actionable, reassuring language.

6.6 **Building Confidence Through Continuous Practice**

Like any skill, becoming proficient in prompting and framing requires practice. With each interaction, take note of what works and what doesn't, refining your approach over time. Here are some ways to build confidence:

Experiment Regularly: Try new approaches, even if they don't always succeed. Experimenting helps reveal what techniques resonate with AI.

Keep a Journal: Document different prompts, framing methods, and outcomes to see patterns and learn from past experiences.

Reflect on Progress: Take time to reflect on how your AI skills have evolved. This not only boosts confidence but also reinforces successful strategies.

6.7 **Practical Tips for Skilled AI Communication**

Here are some final tips for mastering AI communication:

1. Stay Curious: AI is constantly evolving, and so are techniques for interacting with it. Stay open to learning new strategies and adapting to advancements.

2. Be Patient: Not every response will be perfect on the first try. Embrace a mindset of continuous improvement and approach each interaction as a learning opportunity.

3. Focus on Your Goals: Always return to your original objective. Keeping your goal in mind helps streamline interactions and improves relevance.

4. Use AI as a Partner, Not a Replacement: Remember that AI is a tool that enhances your work, not a substitute for human insight. The best results come from collaboration, where AI assists you but does not replace critical thinking.

Conclusion of Chapter 6: The Path to Mastery

Becoming a skilled AI user is a journey of practice, adaptability, and curiosity. By combining strategic prompting and purposeful framing, you unlock the potential to communicate effectively with AI, shaping responses that are insightful, relevant, and tailored to your needs. Whether you're creating educational materials, crafting business strategies, or exploring creative writing, these skills empower you to work seamlessly with AI.

Chapter 7: Advanced Use Cases for AI in Specialized Fields

With a strong foundation in prompting and framing, it's time to explore advanced applications of AI across specialized fields. In this chapter, we'll examine how to apply your skills in contexts that require nuanced communication, creativity, and strategic insight. Whether you're using AI in marketing, education, healthcare, or creative industries, mastering specific use cases can help you unlock even greater value from your interactions.

7.1 **Marketing and Content Creation**

In marketing, AI can enhance customer engagement, streamline content creation, and provide data-driven insights. However, achieving these results requires prompts and framing that cater to audience engagement, brand voice, and strategic goals.

Use Case: Developing Targeted Campaigns

AI can help brainstorm ideas, generate copy, and refine strategies for targeted campaigns. Start by framing the AI's role as a marketing strategist and defining your audience, tone, and objectives.

Example Prompt: "Imagine you're a marketing strategist helping a wellness brand launch a social media campaign for a new line of eco-friendly products. Create three campaign ideas that appeal to eco-conscious millennials and emphasize sustainability."

Expected Outcome: The AI might suggest concepts like user-generated content campaigns, educational posts on sustainability, or product giveaways that encourage eco-friendly habits.

Use Case: Writing Brand-Specific Content

Writing content that aligns with a brand's identity is key to successful marketing. By framing AI with brand guidelines or specific traits, you can ensure that responses align with the brand's voice and values.

Example Prompt: "Write a blog post introduction for a high-end skincare brand targeting professionals in their 30s and 40s. The tone should be luxurious, informative, and emphasize self-care benefits."

Expected Outcome: The AI will likely produce a refined introduction focusing on the brand's quality, benefits for professionals, and a tone that resonates with an upscale audience.

7.2 Education and Instructional Design

In education, AI can be an asset for creating accessible and engaging learning materials, as well as for providing feedback and support to students. By specifying age level, subject matter, and instructional goals, you can frame responses that are educationally sound and tailored to the needs of students.

Use Case: Simplifying Complex Concepts

AI can break down challenging topics into digestible pieces. For younger students or beginners, framing prompts for age-appropriate language and relatable examples is crucial.

Example Prompt: "Explain the basics of the water cycle to a 6th-grade science class. Use simple language and include an analogy that makes it easy to understand."

Expected Outcome: The AI might describe the water cycle in terms of everyday weather events, comparing it to how a sponge soaks up and releases water, making it more relatable for young learners.

Use Case: Generating Study Materials

Teachers can use AI to generate flashcards, quizzes, and discussion questions. By framing prompts with clear educational objectives, you can create materials that align with curriculum goals.

Example Prompt: "Create five discussion questions for high school students about Shakespeare's 'Macbeth,' focusing on themes of ambition and morality."

Expected Outcome: The AI will produce questions that prompt critical thinking, such as, "How does Macbeth's ambition influence his decisions, and what are the moral consequences?"

7.3 Healthcare Communication and Support

In healthcare, AI has the potential to improve patient communication, provide educational resources, and assist with mental health support. However, healthcare prompts must be framed carefully to ensure accuracy, empathy, and adherence to ethical guidelines.

Use Case: Patient Education

AI can create educational materials that help patients understand their conditions, treatment options, and self-care practices. Framing responses with empathy and simplicity ensures patients feel supported.

Example Prompt: "Imagine you're a nurse explaining diabetes management to a newly diagnosed adult patient. Provide a friendly and supportive overview that covers diet, exercise, and medication basics."

Expected Outcome: The AI might offer an approachable guide that balances important information with encouragement, making the patient feel informed and empowered.

Use Case: Mental Health Support and Resources

For mental health applications, prompts should prioritize sensitivity and positive reinforcement. Framing responses for empathy and encouragement can help AI deliver supportive guidance for individuals seeking advice or coping strategies.

Example Prompt: "Imagine you're a counselor helping someone cope with anxiety. Provide gentle advice on daily practices they can use to manage stress."

Expected Outcome: The AI may suggest practical, soothing techniques, such as deep breathing, mindfulness, and breaking down tasks, helping the person feel grounded and supported.

7.4 Creative Industries: Writing, Art, and Entertainment

Creative professionals can use AI to generate ideas, develop characters, and even create art concepts. By framing for genre, style, and tone, you can harness AI's potential to inspire original content or explore new creative directions.

Use Case: Character Development in Writing

AI can help writers flesh out character traits, motivations, and backstories, making it a valuable tool for narrative development. Providing specific genre or personality details can help the AI produce vivid, compelling character profiles.

Example Prompt: "Create a character profile for a science fiction novel. The character is a rebellious space explorer with a hidden past and a strong sense of justice."

Expected Outcome: The AI might generate a complex character with specific personality traits, skills, and motivations, providing a foundation for further development.

Use Case: Visual Art and Concept Development

AI can also assist visual artists in brainstorming concepts and exploring themes. Framing AI responses for specific artistic styles or themes can result in visually engaging ideas that fit the desired mood.

Example Prompt: "Describe an art concept for a surrealist painting that depicts a dream-like cityscape merging with nature."

Expected Outcome: The AI could describe scenes where buildings dissolve into trees, rivers flow through streets, or animals roam in an urban landscape, offering inspiration for a surreal artwork.

7.5 Business Strategy and Data Analysis

For business professionals, AI can assist in strategic planning, market analysis, and data interpretation. With well-framed prompts, AI can offer insights that support data-driven decision-making and problem-solving.

Use Case: Market Analysis

AI can help identify trends and opportunities within specific markets. By framing prompts to focus on particular industries or consumer behaviors, the response can provide actionable insights.

Example Prompt: "Analyze current trends in the eco-friendly consumer product market and suggest three opportunities for growth that a small business could pursue."

Expected Outcome: The AI may identify trends like sustainable packaging, eco-conscious branding, or local sourcing, offering insights tailored to a small business context.

Use Case: Decision-Making and Problem-Solving

AI can provide a strategic perspective on business challenges. When framed for a specific problem, AI can analyze options and suggest potential solutions.

Example Prompt: "Imagine you're a consultant advising a startup facing cash flow issues. Outline three short-term strategies to improve cash flow."

Expected Outcome: The AI could suggest strategies like optimizing inventory, reducing non-essential expenses, or renegotiating payment terms, providing practical steps for immediate improvement.

7.6 **Tips for Mastering Specialized Use Cases**

To make the most of AI in specialized fields, keep the following tips in mind:

1. Specify the Industry or Field: The more detail you provide about the field, the more relevant the response. Tailoring prompts for industry-specific language and needs enhances accuracy and utility.

2. Define the Audience: Understanding who the content is for—whether it's clients, students, patients, or consumers—helps

shape responses that resonate with the intended audience.

3. Consider Ethical and Legal Implications: In areas like healthcare, business, or finance, be mindful of ethical and legal considerations. Frame prompts to avoid advice that could be interpreted as professional, medical, or legal counsel without a disclaimer.

4. Use Iteration to Refine Outputs: Complex tasks may require multiple iterations to achieve the best result. Refine prompts step-by-step, reviewing each response and adjusting as needed to fine-tune the outcome.

7.7 **Practice Exercises: Specialized Use Cases**

Here are exercises to help you practice specialized use cases, using prompts and framing to achieve specific goals:

1. Marketing: "Imagine you're creating a campaign for a sustainable fashion brand targeting young adults. Suggest three campaign ideas that emphasize ethical sourcing and eco-friendly practices."

2. Education: "Explain Newton's laws of motion in simple language, as if you're teaching a 10th-grade physics class, with examples that relate to everyday life."

3. Healthcare: "Provide empathetic advice to someone who recently experienced a job loss. Offer practical coping strategies to help them manage stress and maintain a positive outlook."

4. Creative Writing: "Create an outline for a mystery novel where the protagonist is an amateur detective with a background in psychology. Include major plot points and character motivations."

5. Business Strategy: "Advise a small tech startup on three effective ways to differentiate their product in a competitive market."

Conclusion of Chapter 7: Expanding Your AI Skills in Specialized Fields

Using AI in specialized fields opens up new possibilities for creativity, efficiency, and insight. By applying tailored prompts and framing, you can achieve responses that are specific, relevant, and impactful, suited to the demands of each unique field. With practice, you'll be able to leverage AI as a powerful tool, no matter the industry or goal.

Chapter 8: Troubleshooting and Refining Your AI Techniques

As you become more advanced in using AI, you may encounter situations where responses don't quite meet your expectations. This chapter focuses on troubleshooting common issues, providing strategies for refining your prompts, and discussing advanced techniques to ensure productive interactions with AI. Understanding how to troubleshoot effectively will empower you to overcome roadblocks and continue improving the quality of AI responses.

8.1 Recognizing Common Challenges

Even experienced AI users may face occasional challenges when generating responses. Let's explore some common issues and identify their possible causes:

1. Generic Responses: Sometimes, the AI might produce responses that feel overly broad or lack depth. This often happens if the prompt is too general or doesn't provide enough framing for context.

2. Irrelevant or Off-Topic Answers: When the AI's response doesn't address your core question, it's usually because the prompt was unclear or the framing misled the AI.

3. Inconsistent Tone: If the tone feels too casual, too formal, or simply doesn't match your expectations, it could be due to a lack of guidance on the desired style or audience.

4. Incomplete Answers: Sometimes, responses may only partially answer your question or skip important details. This

can result from overly complex or compound prompts that leave gaps in AI understanding.

8.2 **Troubleshooting Techniques**

Let's look at some practical troubleshooting techniques for refining your prompts and framing to overcome these issues.

Issue 1: Generic Responses

Solution: Be Specific and Add Layers of Framing

If the response lacks detail, consider refining your prompt with additional specifics, including details like audience, purpose, or style.

Original Prompt: "Explain the importance of mental health."

Refined Prompt: "Explain the importance of mental health for young professionals managing high-stress jobs. Include practical self-care strategies they can use."

The refined prompt gives the AI a clearer direction, prompting a response that is more tailored and useful.

Issue 2: Irrelevant or Off-Topic Answers

Solution: Break Down and Focus the Prompt

If the AI's answer doesn't stay on topic, your prompt may be too broad or compound. Try breaking it down into smaller parts and focusing on one aspect at a time.

Original Prompt: "Explain climate change and how it affects the economy, people, and wildlife."

Refined Prompts:

"Explain the economic impact of climate change."

"Describe how climate change affects human populations."

"Discuss the effects of climate change on wildlife."

Breaking down complex prompts ensures that each aspect is thoroughly addressed.

Issue 3: Inconsistent Tone

Solution: Define Tone and Style Clearly in the Framing

When the tone doesn't match your intent, add clear instructions on the tone and style you want the AI to adopt.

Original Prompt: "Write a welcome email for new customers."

Refined Prompt: "Write a professional yet friendly welcome email for new customers, introducing them to our brand and providing a special offer."

By specifying "professional yet friendly," the refined prompt guides the AI to adopt an appropriate tone.

Issue 4: Incomplete Answers

Solution: Simplify the Prompt or Request a Step-by-Step Response

If the AI's response feels incomplete, try simplifying the prompt or requesting a step-by-step answer to ensure each point is covered.

Original Prompt: "How can a business improve productivity, manage finances better, and attract new clients?"

Refined Prompt: "List three ways a business can improve productivity."

Followed by: "Suggest three strategies for better financial management in a business."

Followed by: "Offer three ideas for attracting new clients to a business."

By addressing each area individually, you're more likely to get detailed, thorough answers for each point.

8.3 Advanced Refinement Techniques

Once you've mastered the basics of troubleshooting, these advanced refinement techniques can help you fine-tune your interactions for optimal results.

Technique 1: Test Variations of Prompts

For complex tasks, try generating several variations of a prompt to compare responses. Sometimes, even slight changes in wording can lead to vastly different answers. Experimentation is key to discovering which version yields the best outcome.

Example Variations:

"Provide five tips for improving productivity in a remote work environment."

"Suggest strategies to increase productivity for remote workers facing home distractions."

"How can remote workers stay productive despite common home distractions?"

By comparing responses, you'll find the phrasing that best aligns with your goals.

Technique 2: Provide Examples Within the Prompt

If you're seeking a specific format or style, providing examples within your prompt can guide the AI in replicating that structure.

Example Prompt: "Write a short introduction for an article on work-life balance. For reference, here's a sample style: 'Balancing work and personal life is no easy feat, but with a few practical steps, it's achievable for anyone.' Now, create a similar introduction for our topic."

This gives the AI a model to follow, resulting in a response that matches your stylistic expectations more closely.

Technique 3: Use Follow-Up Prompts for Refinement

Sometimes, you may not get the perfect answer on the first try, but follow-up prompts can refine the initial response. Think of this as a conversation in which each additional prompt clarifies your intent.

Initial Prompt: "Summarize the benefits of meditation."

Follow-Up Prompt: "Add more detail on how meditation affects focus and concentration."

Each follow-up prompt narrows the response to ensure it fully covers your specific needs.

8.4 Practice Exercises: Troubleshooting and Refining

Here are some practice prompts and troubleshooting steps to help you refine your skills. Review the initial prompt, consider the desired outcome, and experiment with adjustments to improve clarity and depth.

1. Initial Prompt: "Explain the importance of teamwork."

Refinement Needed: Add specific context and audience.

Refined Prompt: "Explain the importance of teamwork for new employees in a fast-paced tech company. Include how it contributes to innovation and problem-solving."

2. Initial Prompt: "Describe how AI can help in healthcare."

Refinement Needed: Focus on a specific area within healthcare.

Refined Prompt: "Describe how AI can assist in diagnosing and managing chronic illnesses, highlighting the potential benefits for patient care."

3. Initial Prompt: "Write a sales email."

Refinement Needed: Specify product, audience, and tone.

Refined Prompt: "Write a persuasive sales email promoting a productivity app to small business owners. The tone should be professional and emphasize the app's efficiency benefits."

8.5 Tips for Building Confidence in Troubleshooting

Troubleshooting is an ongoing skill, and it's natural to encounter trial and error as you refine your prompts. Here are some tips to build confidence:

Don't Settle for the First Response: AI responses can improve with each iteration, so don't hesitate to refine your prompts until you're satisfied.

Be Patient and Persistent: Effective AI communication is a skill developed through practice and persistence. With each interaction, you'll gain insights that lead to better responses.

Reflect on Progress: Keep a record of successful prompts and framing strategies. Reflecting on what works helps reinforce effective techniques and encourages a continuous learning mindset.

8.6 Real-World Scenarios: Troubleshooting in Practice

Let's look at some real-world scenarios where troubleshooting and refining techniques can lead to better outcomes.

Scenario 1: Developing an Online Course

Goal: Create engaging, structured content for an online course on digital marketing.

Initial Prompt: "Create an outline for a digital marketing course."

Issue: Too broad, leading to a generic outline.

Refined Prompt: "Create an outline for a beginner-level digital marketing course for small business owners, focusing on social media and email marketing."

Outcome: The refined prompt guides the AI to create a more specific outline suited to beginners and small businesses.

Scenario 2: Writing a Product Description

Goal: Write a persuasive, detailed description for a new kitchen gadget.

Initial Prompt: "Describe a new blender."

Issue: Too vague, leading to a generic response.

Refined Prompt: "Write a product description for a high-speed blender designed for busy parents. Highlight its time-saving features, ease of cleaning, and versatility."

Outcome: The refined prompt results in a response that speaks directly to the target audience and highlights the product's unique benefits.

Scenario 3: Crafting an FAQ Section

Goal: Develop an FAQ section for a website that sells eco-friendly home products.

Initial Prompt: "Create FAQ questions."

Issue: Lacks specific product focus, leading to general questions.

Refined Prompt: "Create an FAQ section for a website that sells eco-friendly cleaning products. Include questions on ingredients, sustainability, and packaging."

Outcome: The refined prompt guides the AI to create relevant, detailed FAQ questions tailored to the product's unique aspects.

Conclusion of Chapter 8: Mastering Troubleshooting and Refinement

Troubleshooting and refining are essential skills for achieving high-quality interactions with AI. By recognizing common issues, experimenting with prompt adjustments, and practicing advanced techniques, you can consistently improve the relevance, accuracy, and depth of AI responses. The ability to troubleshoot effectively transforms AI from a basic tool into a highly adaptable

Conclusion: Mastering AI Communication for Powerful Results

Throughout this book, we've explored the art and science of communicating with AI—understanding prompts, framing for clarity, and refining techniques to achieve accurate, relevant responses. What started as a basic introduction to prompting evolved into an advanced skill set, empowering you to use AI across diverse fields, from education and marketing to healthcare and creative arts.

Mastering AI communication requires a blend of creativity, precision, and adaptability. Simple adjustments, like specifying your audience or adding context, can make the difference between a generic response and one that truly resonates with your needs. With each prompt and frame, you shape the AI's understanding, guiding it to provide nuanced insights, vivid storytelling, or actionable strategies. But beyond technical skills, effective AI communication is about collaboration. AI becomes most powerful when you use it as a partner, combining its strengths in data processing and consistency with your unique perspective and judgment. Together, this collaboration can produce outcomes that are both efficient and deeply insightful.

The journey of mastering AI communication doesn't end here. With AI technology constantly evolving, your skills will continue to grow as you practice, experiment, and adapt to new capabilities. Embrace a mindset of continuous learning and don't shy away from exploring new possibilities. Every interaction is an opportunity to refine your approach, discover new applications, and unlock even greater potential.

As you move forward, remember that AI communication is as much an art as it is a science. Approach it with curiosity, patience, and an open mind. Whether you're solving problems, sparking creativity, or providing support, you now have the tools to make AI an impactful and integral part of your work. The future of AI holds exciting opportunities, and with your mastery of prompting and framing, you're well-prepared to make the most of them.